101 WAYS TO STOP LOSING YOUR CUSTOMERS

Deliver Five Star Service At Any Level

Vivian Campbell

101 Ways To Stop Losing Your Customers: Deliver Five Star Service At Any Level
Campbell, Vivian

ISBN: 978-1-70420-448-2

Published by:
10-10-10 Publishing
Markham, Ontario

First 10-10-10 Publishing paperback edition November 2019

Contents

I dedicate this book to every business owner
who is struggling with customer service issues.

And of course, I dedicate this book to
my loving and supportive mother and father.

Foreword

Vivian Campbell's title says it all. *101 Ways To Stop Losing Your Customers* is exactly what your establishment needs today.

Vivian has been in the hospitality industry for over 20 years. She has opened hotels and trained employees on how to execute great customer service. She understands what a client wants and how to anticipate their needs and then deliver above their expectations. And after reading her book, you will understand as well!

Vivian's delightful yet sarcastic humor makes the point in each one of her scenarios. Her tips on how to deliver five star service at any level are simple and easy to follow. Sometimes you might forget about the basics, and this book is a great reminder.

If you are a business owner who is struggling with low customer satisfaction scores, and you want to improve and increase your repeat business, this book is a must read!

Raymond Aaron
New York Times Bestselling Author

Acknowledgements

I would like to acknowledge my publisher, **Raymond Aaron,** and my personal book architect, **Naval Kumar**. Without your guidance and support, this book would not have been completed.

Thank you to my fabulous **BNI Breakfast Club** for your comradery, weekly shenanigans, and support.

Thank you to **Robert Draney, Mark Harada,** and **Jim McPartlin** for being such gracious and positive leaders in my life. I have learned so much from each of you.

Thank you to **Jean Grant, Joan Yordy, Phil Jun, Julie Logan, Tess Maribao,** and **Debbie Goldfarb** for always being available to be my sounding board.

Thank you to my BFF's: **Theodore X Garcia, Rupert Grant,** and **Romualdo Teh** for your support and friendship over the decades. Thank you to **Master Ken Nagayama, Ms Kimberly Moulton,** and **Mr. Amon Platis** for your guidance and support over the years. I am even stronger from all of your teachings.

Thank you **God** and **Father Ed Benioff** for spiritual guidance every day, especially on Sunday mornings, and for always reminding me to be humble and to help others.

Thank you to my loving parents, **Mary and Joseph Campbell**. That's right, Mary and Joseph! Your never ending love and support has always been and will always be much appreciated.

Chapter 1

Welcome

What is going on with our customer service today? It is just awful. No one wants to tip for bad service, but the majority of us do it anyway, simply because we don't want to look bad. Kudos to those of you who don't tip when you get bad service, and you don't give a damn if anyone knows it!

I have worked in the hospitality industry for 15 years as I write this book. My observations have become more in tune, as I am a member of the industry who must always deliver exceptional service. Sometimes I have delivered amazing service, sometimes phenomenal, while other times simply good service. I believe that the type of service we get at an establishment comes from the experience, training, and management of that establishment.

I will give you examples of what actually happened to customers, and then share with you WHAT SHOULD HAVE HAPPENED for the customer. I am sure most of you will be able to relate to these examples because, unfortunately for you and me, customer service sucks nowadays. And we shouldn't take it anymore!

If you think about it, customer service is really fairly simple. Here's what happens if we, as the customer, are lucky. An employee with a pleasing personality gets hired, trained, and put into play. Now, what should actually happen is the employee with the pleasing personality is put through an on- boarding process where they will spend anywhere from 15–60 minutes with various departments they will interact with. This way, the employees get to know each other, and they know what they should expect and deliver as colleagues. Next, once the employee is trained, they should shadow a senior employee before being put into play. After they shadow someone, that person should shadow them, and only once they pass a checklist of items that they must know from their training, do they finally get to be put in play on their own. This process should take however long it takes. All the steps need to be satisfied and signed off by the supervising manager and the employee so that they are both in agreement on what is expected and what will be delivered.

After the employee is put into play, they should be monitored daily for a minimum of one week, and then a one on one should be done every other week, even if only for 15 minutes, to stay in tune with each other on work performance, as well as building a solid rapport.

This book will illustrate that 101 businesses are losing their customers when this training process does not happen.

Enjoy the read.

Chapter 2

Restaurants – Table for 2?

"A lot of restaurants serve good food,
but they don't have very good service."
– Wolfgang Puck

All of us at one time or another has gone out to eat. As dining customers, we should all receive good service. It doesn't matter if we are eating at a burger joint or a Michelin 3-star restaurant. There are basic customer service expectations for all levels.

Customers want a clean restaurant, good food, and a pleasant experience. The key, of course, is communication. This can't be over emphasized. There needs to be communication amongst the team. The bartender, bus boy, food runner, and manager are there to help the server provide the best service possible.

ARRIVAL

SCENARIO 1: MIA at the front desk.

A pair of hungry diners walk into a restaurant. When no one approaches, the couple turn into amateur detectives. They look around. They try to make eye contact with someone who can help, but it's not working. What to do? Should they seat themselves? Do they stay there and wait? Or do they just . . . walk out?

A CUSTOMER COMMENTS

"I get impatient and aggravated when I walk into a place to eat and no one notices. I have come to eat your food and give you money, yet no one seems to care. Can you believe it? If I have to get my own menu and find my own seat, I might as well go in the kitchen and cook my own food!"

RATING: You've got to be kidding me@%! | Seriously?! | OMG! | *Really?* | #Love that

WHAT SHOULD HAVE HAPPENED

If the host steps away to seat another party, or for any other reason, the rest of the team needs to keep an eye on the door. The servers with tables closest to this area, and the bartender or any other staff member in proximity, should greet guests coming in. First impressions are everything. There should always be someone to greet a guest the moment they arrive. The guest experience begins here and sets the tone for the rest of the diner's visit. – *#Love that*

*****

SCENARIO 2: Guests didn't get the table they were promised.

A guest books a table at a restaurant to celebrate a friend's birthday. He makes the reservation, specifically asking for a table with a view. The restaurant confirms his booking and does not mention any problem. His party arrives a few minutes early, only to have the host indifferently inform them that they can either take a different table or wait for the table with a view.

A CUSTOMER COMMENTS

"I had a reservation for a table with a view, which was confirmed. What happened? Our "special" table is one of our favorite things about this restaurant, but it's pretty much spoiled now."

RATING: You've got to be kidding me@%! | *Seriously?!* | OMG! | Really? | #Love that

WHAT SHOULD HAVE HAPPENED

When a guest calls ahead to reserve a particular table, it needs to be communicated to anyone else who may be at the host stand, to make sure it happens. A note on the reservation isn't a bad idea either. If there's a mix up, and a customer's request can't be honored, there should be an immediate apology for the mistake—even better, an offer to buy their party a cocktail while they wait for the table they requested. – *#Love that*

*****   .

SCENARIO 3: The host is unhelpful.
The host seats the guest, drops the menu, and moves away as quickly as possible. The bewildered diner catches the host and asks for water. The host snaps back, "Ask your server."

A CUSTOMER COMMENTS
"So you only have the one job of seating us, and that's it? You're not allowed or willing to do anything else for us?"

RATING: You've got to be kidding me@%! | *Seriously?!* | OMG! | Really? | #Love that

WHAT SHOULD HAVE HAPPENED
When the host is seating a party, he or she should hand each person a menu, with the company logo facing the diner. The host should make sure that silverware is on the table. A lovely *"Enjoy your meal"* is always appropriate. And if the guest requests anything right off the bat, the host should tell them that they would gladly get it for them. It's called teamwork. – *#Love that*

*****

SCENARIO 4: The hostess blatantly lies.

Have you ever caught a staff member lying? You reserve a window table and, after waiting 30 minutes, the hostess seats you at a regular table. When you explain that you were promised a window table, she says that the last one is reserved for a friend of the owner. After the party arrives at the window table, you ask in a cordial manner how they know the owner. They say that they don't know the owner. Busted!

A CUSTOMER COMMENTS

"Lying is never okay. Someone dropped the ball on your reservation, and they were covering up their mistake with a lie that they think you won't find out about."

RATING: *You've got to be kidding me@%!* | Seriously?! | OMG! | Really? | #Love that

WHAT SHOULD HAVE HAPPENED

Lying is a major violation of the customer's trust. A customer who has been lied to will likely never come back (and spread the word on social media too). If the host made a mistake, they should be honest about it, and then make it right with a free cocktail (or two!). – *#Love that*

*****

SCENARIO 5: Guests are seated at a dirty table.

The restaurant is packed, and the only free table still has food and dirty dishes on it, along with food bits on the floor, and crumbs on the chairs. A group of diners has to stand there and wait while the hostess runs to get a bus boy to clean the table.

A CUSTOMER COMMENTS

"Why on earth would you bring guests to a dirty table? If I wanted a pile of dirty dishes, I could've stayed home."

RATING: You've got to be kidding me@%! | *Seriously?!* | OMG! | Really? | #Love that

WHAT SHOULD HAVE HAPPENED

Before taking a guest to a table, it should be completely bussed, cleaned, and ready for service. All unnecessary items should be cleared, such as ketchup, syrup, and hot sauce. In short, the hostess should be communicating with the servers and bussers *before* seating a customer. – *#Love that*

*****

DURING THE MEAL

SCENARIO 6: Food allergies are not taken seriously.

A customer asks the server and is told that the sangria does not have mango. However, the server doesn't say it with much confidence, so the guest asks someone else—and, lo and behold, it does. The guest then asks the manager, and he confirms the ingredients. But no one really seems to mind that a customer could have become extremely ill, had he not done the extra legwork.

A CUSTOMER COMMENTS

"Uh, does the staff understand how bad my food allergies can be for me? For example, if I eat anything even remotely related to peanuts or peanut oil, I could go into anaphylactic shock, and potentially DIE."

RATING: *You've got to be kidding me@%!* | Seriously?! | OMG! | Really? | #Love that

WHAT SHOULD HAVE HAPPENED

Food allergies should be covered in depth during training for all servers, and they should know all of the ingredients and available substitutions, before they are permitted on the floor. When the server is notified of an allergy, they should speak directly to the kitchen, to confirm the ingredients if they are at all unsure. – *#Love that*

✶✶✶✶✶

SCENARIO 7: Guests are ignored after being seated.
The hostess seats a couple right away but doesn't give them a menu. As the customers sit there without a menu or a glass of water, it's another 10 minutes before the server even acknowledges them, and that was only because the pair managed to flag him down.

A CUSTOMER COMMENTS
"Hello, people! I am here, hungry, and ready to give you my money! Where are you?"

RATING: You've got to be kidding me@%! | Seriously?! | *OMG!* | Really? | #Love that

WHAT SHOULD HAVE HAPPENED
Communication among team members is key. The host should inform the guest of their server's name, and then let them know that they will be with them shortly—and a lovely *"Enjoy your meal"* wouldn't hurt either. If the server is obviously backed up, providing a menu to keep the customer busy isn't such a hard concept. The host needs to have the server's back. – *#Love that*

*****

SCENARIO 8: The server doesn't introduce him/herself.

The server comes over to your table, stares at his notepad, and asks, "May I take your order?"

A CUSTOMER COMMENTS
"Maybe we can start with your name and a welcome? Are there any specials we should know about? Dude, you have already gone to second base, and we are still on first."

RATING: You've got to be kidding me@%! | Seriously?! | OMG! | *Really?* | #Love that

WHAT SHOULD HAVE HAPPENED
The server should introduce themselves and offer a greeting, such as, "Good evening, have you dined with us before?" followed by, "Can I tell you about our specials?" or "Do you have any questions about the menu?" – *#Love that*

*****

SCENARIO 9: There is wine but no glasses.

A carafe of water or wine appears on the table but with no accompanying glassware. It's the same as getting a tray of appetizers but no plates.

A CUSTOMER COMMENTS

"I know family-style is really in right now, but we can't all drink from the same carafe!"

RATING: You've got to be kidding me@%! | Seriously?! | OMG! | ***Really?*** | #Love that

WHAT SHOULD HAVE HAPPENED

When food and beverages are brought to a table, the server needs to make sure that the table has all the tools they need for an enjoyable meal. In other words, napkins, glassware, china, and silverware. Those should already be on the table when the food is delivered. If it isn't, the food runner had better get those items to the table ASAP. — *#Love that*

*****

SCENARIO 10: The server doesn't know… well, anything.
Have you ever been in the process of ordering, and you have some basic questions about the menu items? Every time you ask the server a simple question, he replies, "I'm not sure."

A CUSTOMER COMMENTS
"Perhaps I can get another server who can actually assist me with my order."

RATING: You've got to be kidding me@%! | *Seriously?!* | OMG! | Really? | #Love that

WHAT SHOULD HAVE HAPPENED
The server should always be prepared to explain any menu items: preparation, ingredients, temperatures, and any other information a customer might need. If the server is not trained to do this, he should not be permitted on the floor. – *#Love that*

*****

SCENARIO 11: The server is a sad sack.

Have you ever had bad service from a server who seemed to be miserable working there? She not only provides awful service but she gives a lot of attitude. She is not attentive at all. You ask for the wine menu three times because she keeps forgetting. She even rolls her eyes after receiving a complaint about the cold coffee during dessert.

A CUSTOMER COMMENTS

"I know that restaurants make a lot of their money from alcohol sales, so it is surprising to neglect repeated requests for a wine menu. And this attitude has got to go."

RATING: You've got to be kidding me@%! | Seriously?! | *OMG!* | Really? | #Love that

WHAT SHOULD HAVE HAPPENED

If a server is having a bad day, they should pull it together or go home. If it's possible, they need to get someone to cover their tables, and take a break. Then they need to get back in there and give their full attention to their tables. – *#Love that*

✶✶✶✶✶

SCENARIO 12: The server has her head in the clouds.

Have you ever had a very pleasant server that was just preoccupied? You order salads and dinner, and after the salads are cleared, time goes by, and she shows up and offers you dessert? I guess skipping the entrée portion of the meal is one way to speed things along!

A CUSTOMER COMMENTS

"Someone is truly not paying attention. Were the entrées even ordered? Aren't they in the window, waiting to be picked up?"

RATING: You've got to be kidding me@%! | Seriously?! | OMG! | *Really?* | #Love that

WHAT SHOULD HAVE HAPPENED

Servers are supposed to be checking in on their tables throughout the meal. If they are, then they will always know which course you are on. Being preoccupied is no excuse. – *#Love that*

✶✶✶✶✶

SCENARIO 13: The server is rude.

Have you ever taken your friends to one of your favorite restaurants, and then you are completely embarrassed because the service is disappointing? The server is apparently having a bad day. They are rude and impatient. When the bill is presented, there is a snide message scribbled on the bill.

A CUSTOMER COMMENTS

"Who does this? Are you asking to be fired? You can't leave nasty messages on the bill that you give to your guests."

RATING: You've got to be kidding me@%! | Seriously?! | OMG! | ***Really?*** | #Love that

WHAT SHOULD HAVE HAPPENED

Floor managers should be checking in on the tables to make sure guests are having a wonderful time. They should also be touching base with the wait staff, to make sure they are okay and that things are going well with their tables. If good communication is taking place amongst the team, the nasty note situation is a lot less likely to happen. – *#Love that*

*****

SCENARIO 14: The server is inexperienced—very inexperienced.

Have you ever had a server who was extremely inexperienced? He serves you bread that is cold and stale. You track him down and ask for some fresh bread. He informs you that this bread is all they have, and there's nothing he can do.

A CUSTOMER COMMENTS

"Um, so you're not going to even try to offer us something better? We are just kinda done with this request?"

RATING: You've got to be kidding me@%! | Seriously?! | *OMG!* | Really? | #Love that

WHAT SHOULD HAVE HAPPENED

The fault here lies with the manager, because this server was not properly trained. If a guest is unhappy with something, the server should be trained to ask for help, not just tell the customer "tough luck." If a food item is unacceptable, it should be replaced immediately, and an apology given. – *#Love that*

*****

SCENARIO 15: The server doesn't know who ordered what.

Have you ever been to a restaurant where they "auction off" your food when it arrives at the table? You know what I mean; when the food arrives, and the person delivering it has no clue who ordered what. "Now, who gets the fish?" and "I've got pasta here."

A CUSTOMER COMMENTS

"The server should know who ordered which dish. Is that information somehow top secret?"

RATING: You've got to be kidding me@%! | Seriously?! | OMG! | *Really?* | #Love that

WHAT SHOULD HAVE HAPPENED

When the server takes the order, they should indicate what seat position it belongs to. This information should be shared with the food runners. Entrees should be placed in front of each guest without all the commentary. – *#Love that*

*****

SCENARIO 16: The plate is chipped.

Have you ever received your food and noticed that your plate is chipped? You mention this to the server, and he says he will make a note of it.

A CUSTOMER COMMENTS

"Thanks! How about taking the plate of food back and making sure that part of the plate isn't in it before re-plating my food?"

RATING: You've got to be kidding me@%! | Seriously?! | OMG! | *Really?* | #Love that

WHAT SHOULD HAVE HAPPENED

Three people should have seen this plate before it came out to the table. If by chance the plate got chipped on the way out of the kitchen, it should have been caught when the plate was put down on the table, and immediately removed. In any case, a chipped plate is not acceptable. – *#Love that*

*****

SCENARIO 17: The order is wrong.
Have you ever had food brought to the table, and your order was wrong? Instead of the server apologizing, he blames the kitchen for the mistake. You're not really sure where the mistake happened, but what difference does it make? You just want the food you ordered.

A CUSTOMER COMMENTS
"Blaming your coworkers in front of the customer is never appropriate."

RATING: You've got to be kidding me@%! | Seriously?! | *OMG!* | Really? | #Love that

WHAT SHOULD HAVE HAPPENED
Ideally, a server will always deliver the meal you ordered. But if a mistake does happen, the server should apologize and get it replaced immediately. If the meal cannot be replaced promptly, discount or comp the meal. – *#Love that*

*****

SCENARIO 18: Only half the table gets their entrees.

A group of friends comes in for dinner but only half of the entrees are brought to the table at the same time. Those with their food don't want to dig in while their friends wait for their food. Meanwhile, the meals on the table go cold.

A CUSTOMER COMMENTS

"How does this even happen if the server is checking in on his tables? Whatever happened to checking in on the table to see how everything is tasting? When you have food, it's usually tasting pretty good."

RATING: You've got to be kidding me@%! | Seriously?! | *OMG!* | Really? | #Love that

WHAT SHOULD HAVE HAPPENED

Even if it means holding something back for five minutes in the kitchen, orders should be delivered as closely together as possible, so that the group can eat at the same time. But if a meal is ever slow coming out, the server should acknowledge the delay and inform the guests that the food will be out shortly. This lets the guest know that they were not forgotten. Maybe a free appetizer could be given for the one whose entrée is delayed, so that the others can dig in. And if it's really late? All food needs to come out at the same time. We wouldn't send an appetizer to half the table. – *#Love that*

*****

SCENARIO 19: The server only wants to take the drink order first.
A hungry party of four arrives at their favorite dining spot. They know the menu well, and all have their drink and food orders ready to go. But the server is in such a rush that she takes the drink orders and then disappears without asking if they are ready to order their food.

A CUSTOMER COMMENTS
"You can come back. We won't bite."

RATING: You've got to be kidding me@%! | Seriously?! | OMG! | *Really?* | #Love that

WHAT SHOULD HAVE HAPPENED
Better communication. How about, "Let me put these drink orders in, and I will be right back to take your dinner orders. Oh, you're ready? Great! I'll take your entrée orders now too."
– #Love that

✳✳✳✳✳

SCENARIO 20: The server forgets the birthday cake. A party takes a loved one out for his birthday, and the organizer whispers to the hostess to ask about something sweet, with a candle, at the end of dinner. Agreed. But somehow there is a disconnect because, after the entrees, the server drops the dessert menus on the table, takes the order, and the birthday treat never shows up.

A CUSTOMER COMMENTS
"Happy Birthday to nobody. So much for that special occasion dinner. We won't be back."

RATING: You've got to be kidding me@%! | *Seriously?!* | OMG! | Really? | #Love that

WHAT SHOULD HAVE HAPPENED
Every restaurant provides something special for such occasions. Some restaurants are more elaborate than others, but they nearly always offer a treat. The server should get with the chef and select the appropriate treat. Once the server is alerted to the birthday, he most certainly shouldn't forget all about it. – *#Love that*

*****

SCENARIO 21: The server pets a dog.
Outside, on a restaurant patio where customers are allowed to bring their pets, a server starts petting a dog. Her guests signal her to tell her that they are missing silverware, and she walks right over to the bin to get some—without washing her hands!

A CUSTOMER COMMENTS
"Um, I think I'll get my own silverware; thank you very much."

RATING: *You've got to be kidding me@%!* | Seriously?! |OMG! | Really? | #Love that

WHAT SHOULD HAVE HAPPENED
We love any restaurants who welcome our canine friends and companions (kudos to the French!). But after handling anything other than food or beverages, the server should wash their hands before going back to their tables. This is non-negotiable.
– #Love that

*****

SCENARIO 22: The servers don't wash their hands.
Have you ever been seated in a restaurant, and one of the workers brings in his newborn baby for everyone to see? The servers not only stop taking care of their tables, but they each want to hold the baby. After one of the servers finally realizes that they have been away from their duties too long, they go straight to their tables and start working again.

A CUSTOMER COMMENTS
"What about washing your hands?"

RATING: *You've got to be kidding me@%!* | Seriously?! | OMG! | Really? | #Love that

WHAT SHOULD HAVE HAPPENED
The servers should not stop being attentive to their tables unless they are on break and someone is covering them. After handling anything other than food or beverages, they should wash their hands before assisting their guests. – *#Love that*

✻✻✻✻✻

SCENARIO 23: The server has abandoned the guests.
Have you ever been eating a meal, and you needed something—like sugar for your coffee or ketchup for your fries—but the server never comes back to check on your table? You're frustrated that you don't have what you need to enjoy your meal. Apparently, once the food was delivered, the server thought he was done.

A CUSTOMER COMMENTS
"Once the food has been dropped, the server isn't on break until it's time to drop the check."

RATING: You've got to be kidding me@%! | Seriously?! | OMG! | *Really?* | #Love that

WHAT SHOULD HAVE HAPPENED
Within two minutes or two bites after delivering the entrée, the server should ask the guest how everything is, and if there is anything else they can get them. – *#Love that*

*****

SCENARIO 24: The server is in too big of a rush.

Have you ever been rushed through your meal at a restaurant? I'm talking all appetizers and main courses being served within 15 minutes? Slow service is bad enough. But too-fast service can be equally annoying. When the restaurant has you in and out in 50 minutes, it hardly makes for an enjoyable meal—so much for a relaxing dinner out with friends.

A CUSTOMER COMMENTS

"How rude! I understand that restaurants need to keep tables moving to make a profit; but I didn't arrive 10 minutes before closing, so there's no excuse to be rushed by the wait staff."

RATING: You've got to be kidding me@%! | Seriously?! | OMG! | ***Really?*** | #Love that

WHAT SHOULD HAVE HAPPENED

The server shouldn't fire all the food at the same time. Appetizers, entrees, and desserts should arrive appropriately spaced so that customers enjoy their meal and want to come back. – *#Love that*

*****

SCENARIO 25: Another server isn't willing to help.
A customer needs red pepper for her *Spaghetti Bolognese*. She flags down a server and tells him exactly what she needs. He replies, "Let me get your server for you." A few minutes later, the original server comes over and asks what the guest wanted. Meanwhile, the spaghetti has grown cold.

A CUSTOMER COMMENTS
"Where's the logic here? It took longer for you to bring over my server, who had me repeat my request, than it would have for you to just do it yourself . . . or for me to do it myself. I can see the red pepper flakes just right over there."

RATING: You've got to be kidding me@%! | Seriously?! | *OMG!* | Really? | #Love that

WHAT SHOULD HAVE HAPPENED
When you are in the business of delivering service, there is no excuse for acting like a customer's need is not "yours," and is not your problem. Instead, the server should have said, "Absolutely." Every server is part of the team. Even if it's not their table, if they are asked for something, they should take ownership of that request. They can also tell a runner, a bus boy, or that specific table's server, but whomever or whatever, just make sure it gets done. *– #Love that*

*****

SCENARIO 26: A guest asks for something, but it never comes. A guest asks for something—maybe some extra sauce or dressing on the side—to enhance his meal. The server says that he'll get it right away, but it never comes.

A CUSTOMER COMMENTS
"I am baffled that so many of my friends experience this. If a few minutes go by, and you still have not received your item, you stop the very next person walking by, and ask someone else. If I ask for something, you better believe I am going to get it."

RATING: You've got to be kidding me@%! | Seriously?! | *OMG!* | Really? | #Love that

WHAT SHOULD HAVE HAPPENED
The server should periodically observe the table throughout the course of the meal. Stop by and ask, "How is everything?" If this is happening, there is no way a customer will feel neglected. Furthermore, all servers should have each other's backs and stay alert for customer signals from every table, not only their own. – *#Love that*

*****

SCENARIO 27: The table piles up with dirty dishes.

Have you ever been in a bar, ordering appetizers? Your table is full of plates, and the server comes by to see how you are doing. You tell her that everything was great, and that you would like to order a few more items. She takes your order and walks away, without removing the dirty plates.

A CUSTOMER COMMENTS

"How do you walk away from a table piled with dirty dishes? Are you going to bring out a sauté pan and just serve us on the plates we already have?"

RATING: You've got to be kidding me@%! | Seriously?! | *OMG!* | Really? | #Love that

WHAT SHOULD HAVE HAPPENED

When a customer finishes eating, and a plate is empty, it should be removed promptly. This should not be left for the busser. – *#Love that*

*****

SCENARIO 28: The food is burned.

Have you ever had a server deliver a plate of food—burned food, literally—that just looked horrible? It made you wonder how it got past the chef in the kitchen.

A CUSTOMER COMMENTS

"I ordered a steak medium rare, not a piece of charcoal burnt to a crisp."

RATING: You've got to be kidding me@%! | Seriously?! | *OMG!* | Really? | #Love that

WHAT SHOULD HAVE HAPPENED

The food should pass through a minimum of three people before it gets to the table: the cook, the expediter, and the server. If you get a plate with burned food, all three should be written up. The customer should get the meal replaced as quickly as possible. *– #Love that*

*****

SCENARIO 29: There are flies in the dessert case.
Have you ever walked into a restaurant where the desserts are in a display case, and you see a fly in there having a field day? You bring this to the attention of the host. He makes a half-hearted attempt to get the fly out, and after a few tries, gives up and moves on to another task.

A CUSTOMER COMMENTS
"Flies? That's disgusting. Is everyone on staff this unconcerned with cleanliness? Do I need to be worried about how safe it is to eat the food I am about to order?"

RATING: You've got to be kidding me@%! | *Seriously?!* | OMG! | Really? | #Love that

WHAT SHOULD HAVE HAPPENED
The host should thank the customer for bringing it to their attention, and then swat at that fly until it's gone. Insects are not something you want to take lightly in the restaurant business. In ideal circumstances, the fly would not be in the case in the first place. – *#Love that*

*****

SCENARIO 30: The server leaves the bill while the guests are still eating.

Have you ever been enjoying your entrée, and your server comes by and drops the bill and walks away? Not only do you feel that you are being dismissed, but you weren't even asked if you wanted to order coffee or dessert.

A CUSTOMER COMMENTS

"Uh... Did I say I was done? Do you need this table? What about dessert and coffee? Does the boss know that you are cutting his sales?"

RATING: You've got to be kidding me@%! | Seriously?! | *OMG!* | Really? | #Love that

WHAT SHOULD HAVE HAPPENED

Only *after* everyone is done eating, and the table is cleared of all plates, should the server ask how everything was, offer dessert or coffee, and bring the bill. – *#Love that*

✳✳✳✳✳

SCENARIO 31: There is coffee but no cream.

Have you ever ordered coffee after dinner, but when the server comes, he doesn't bring you sugar and cream? You ask a couple of other staff people, over a span of 30 minutes, for the items, and you finally get them. By then, the coffee is cold.

A CUSTOMER COMMENTS

"Perhaps the server was serving you coffee they way he likes it: black. You just have to wonder about what type of training is (or isn't) going on when coffee is left at the table without even asking if you wanted cream or sweeteners. It's basic stuff."

RATING: You've got to be kidding me@%! | Seriously?! | OMG! | *Really?* | #Love that

WHAT SHOULD HAVE HAPPENED

Whenever a staff member serves a beverage or food item at a table, they should always make sure that it is complete. In other words, cream and sugar with coffee, ketchup with fries, and honey and sweeteners with hot tea. The server should anticipate the customer's need, or at the very least, ask. – *#Love that*

*****

SCENARIO 32:   Guests are unhappy with their meal, but nobody cares.

Have you ever sent back an entrée because it wasn't cooked properly? Your server seems angry about the request but takes it back to the chef. A few minutes later, she comes back in a huff and says, "We can't remake it for you because it will just come out the same, and we don't want to waste any more money. If you don't want to eat it, you don't have to pay for it."

A CUSTOMER COMMENTS
"Um… are they saying, 'You either eat it, or you can leave?'"

RATING: You've got to be kidding me@%! | Seriously?! | **OMG!** | Really? | #Love that

WHAT SHOULD HAVE HAPPENED
If a guest is unhappy with the meal, it should be replaced immediately. If the customer doesn't like what they ordered, offer them a menu, and replace it with something else. If the meal is not replaced promptly, the meal should be comped. It doesn't matter whose fault it is; it should be taken care of, no questions asked. – *#Love that*

*****

DEPARTURE

SCENARIO 33: The bill is wrong.

After having a great meal, have you ever had the bill come, and the charges are wrong? You're ready to pay out, but now you have to take the time to sort out the mistake.

A CUSTOMER COMMENTS

"OK, mistakes happen, but I think this mistake happens more often than it should."

RATING: You've got to be kidding me@%! | Seriously?! | OMG! | *Really?* | #Love that

WHAT SHOULD HAVE HAPPENED

The server should always double-check their work. It is important to make sure that the bill is correct—every time. – *#Love that*

*****

SCENARIO 34: When the guests leave, no one says a word.
Too often, diners leave a restaurant and no one asks them about their experience, or thanks them for coming in. This happens all the time and, trust me, it leaves a bad taste in the mouth.

A CUSTOMER COMMENTS
"Do you even care that I was here? I left the money on the table, tipped well, and minded my manners. Where are yours?"

RATING: You've got to be kidding me@%! | Seriously?! | OMG! | ***Really?*** | #Love that

WHAT SHOULD HAVE HAPPENED
Someone should always notice guests as they depart, and acknowledge them for choosing your restaurant. A team member should look them in the eye and ask, "How was everything?" or say, "Thanks so much for coming in!" along with an invitation to come back again real soon. *– #Love that*

*****

Chapter 3

Hotels – Checking In?

"I look for the hotels that have figured out the comfortable balance—a modern room that is well designed, and really clean sheets."
– Simon Sinek

Traveling to hotels can be fun. For some of us, it's all work related, but it should still be an enjoyable experience. For those on vacation, you want it to be relaxing and eventful.

Most people want the simple basics when staying at hotels: a clean room, a comfortable bed, good food, good Wi-Fi connection, friendly service, and a feeling of safety.

You want a hotel to exceed your expectations, as opposed to simply providing you good service. Unfortunately for some, they don't receive either.

ARRIVAL

SCENARIO 35: The reservationist accuses you of lying.
Have you ever booked a hotel a month beforehand? You become very ill and can no longer make your trip. You call to inform the hotel, and they seem understanding; and they note that they will let the front desk know. The next day, you call to make sure that you are not being charged for the cancellation, and the reservationist seems to have no interest in your story, and did not even ask how you are doing. She informs you that she did not receive a message, and that she cannot prove that you called and canceled. She insists that you will be charged for the full night, and hangs up.

A CUSTOMER COMMENTS
"Well, who really cares if I live or die? It doesn't really matter because now I am a liar, given the fact that you have no proof. Just because there wasn't a message in your inbox, does that really mean that I didn't call?"

RATING: You've got to be kidding me@%! | Seriously?! | *OMG!* | Really? | #Love that

WHAT SHOULD HAVE HAPPENED
First of all, ask how the guest is feeling. Take some ownership, and investigate further. Perhaps your colleague forgot to leave you a note. – *#Love that*

*****

SCENARIO 36: The hotel shuttle forgets to pick you up.

Have you ever booked car service, from the airport to the hotel, through concierge? You are waiting at the airport after a long flight, and there is no car to be found. It's late and you're tired, so you make other arrangements. You complain, and the person at the five-star hotel says, "I just don't know how that could have happened." You tell them that you do understand that mistakes can happen, but you would appreciate a discount for the mishap. They politely decline.

A CUSTOMER COMMENTS

"Are you for real? I used your services, and they failed. Now you won't take any responsibility to solve this issue?"

RATING: You've got to be kidding me@%! | Seriously?! | *OMG!* | Really? | #Love that

WHAT SHOULD HAVE HAPPENED

First and foremost, offer an apology. Inform the guest that you will find out what happened. In the end, this was a miss on the hotel's part, and some compensation should be offered. – *#Love that*

*****

SCENARIO 37: The hotel website is misleading.

Have you ever checked into your room and looked around, only to find out that your room did not have all the amenities advertised during booking. You call and inform the front desk, where the receptionist tells you that the hotel was booked out due to an event, and that she could not help. You explain to her that the website is deceiving, and that you had chosen the hotel based on the amenities. She tells you that not all the rooms have those amenities, and that they could help you at any other time, but not today. She added, with an irritated and impatient voice, that "everyone has preferences," and that I should be happy because my room was a corner room, and people like the additional space.

A CUSTOMER COMMENTS

"Thanks for pointing out the fact that I have a corner room. I know what I have. I am calling about the items promised on the website, which I don't have."

RATING: You've got to be kidding me@%! | Seriously?! | **OMG!** | Really? | #Love that

WHAT SHOULD HAVE HAPPENED

If you are indeed slammed at the present moment, how about asking the guest if the two of you could kindly review the missing items tomorrow? Ask if there is anything needed right at this moment, and apologize for any inconvenience. – *#Love that*

*****

SCENARIO 38: Your room is already occupied.

Have you ever received keys from the front desk, and you finally get to your room, and the keys don't work? You are by yourself, so you have to take all your luggage back down to get new keys. You lug everything back up and, thank goodness, the key works. You walk into the room and find that it is occupied. You freak out for a moment because someone else may be in the room or coming down the hall back to their room. You know you are violating someone's private space, and you just need to get out of there. You go back to the front desk again, to get a key to another room.

A CUSTOMER COMMENTS

"Can I just see what it says on their screens? Is the field checked "already occupied," in small print and hard to read? Not only is this embarrassing, but it is exhausting with all the back and forth."

RATING: You've got to be kidding me@%! | *Seriously?!* | OMG! | Really? | #Love that

WHAT SHOULD HAVE HAPPENED

First and foremost, offer an apology for the horrible mix up. Double and triple check the new room you are about to assign. Call a bellman to assist the guest up to the room, and follow up with an amenity. – *#Love that*

$$* * * * *$$

SCENARIO 39: The room reeks of fumes.
Have you ever returned to your room to the smell of heavy paint fumes, to the point where you feel nauseous? You call down to find out what is going on in the area. They offer to air out the room when you are out to dinner, and explain that work gets done on rooms, by maintenance, without their knowledge, so they were not sure what happened. You come back after dinner, and it still reeks, and then you realize that a piece of furniture had just been painted!

A CUSTOMER COMMENTS
"Who paints a piece of furniture in an occupied room? Who comes into your room and paints furniture, and doesn't leave a note?"

RATING: *You've got to be kidding me@%!* | Seriously?! | OMG! | Really? | #Love that

WHAT SHOULD HAVE HAPPENED
This one is easy. It should not have happened at all. Hotel staff should not enter an occupied room for maintenance work unless it is an absolute emergency. – *#Love that*

*****

DURING THE STAY

SCENARIO 40: You don't get the room you requested.
Have you ever checked into your room, only to find out that it is the wrong room type? You thought you were getting a king, but you now have two queens. You are pretty sure that you confirmed everything five minutes ago at the front desk, so you are not quite sure what happened. You call downstairs, and you are told that they don't have any more rooms.

A CUSTOMER COMMENTS
"I am pretty sure, when checking in, the front desk agent is stating the type of room you are signing for. So, how do you get keys to a completely different room?"

RATING: You've got to be kidding me@%! | Seriously?! | *OMG!* | Really? | #Love that

WHAT SHOULD HAVE HAPPENED
If the hotel did indeed run out of kings, they should have told you when you were checking in. If they have kings available, they should double check their screens before assigning you your room. They should also have a better understanding of the room types and their corresponding room numbers. – *#Love that*

*****

SCENARIO 41: There's a broom in your room.

Have you ever checked into your room and found a broom and rag, from housekeeping, just sitting there. Now you are looking around your room to see if housekeeping is still in there.

A CUSTOMER COMMENTS

"Am I just supposed to clean up after myself? What is going on here?"

RATING: You've got to be kidding me@%! | ***Seriously?!*** | OMG! | Really? | #Love that

WHAT SHOULD HAVE HAPPENED

The housekeeping manager obviously does not have a good system in place. The sleeping rooms are supposed to be inspected before they get to the front desk for availability. This system obviously failed. – *#Love that*

*****

SCENARIO 42: The front desk won't send up a toothbrush.
Have you ever checked into a hotel, and you unpack your luggage and see that you forgot your toothbrush? You are only staying a couple of nights, so any simple, clean toothbrush will do. You call down to the front desk and tell them that you forgot your toothbrush, and you ask if they have a complimentary toothbrush that you can use. The front desk agent cheerfully says, "Sure, we do. Just stop by the front desk and pick one up."

A CUSTOMER COMMENTS
"Well, he was cheerful."

RATING: You've got to be kidding me@%! | Seriously?! | OMG! | ***Really?*** | #Love that

---

WHAT SHOULD HAVE HAPPENED
The front desk agent should have said, "I will send one up right away." – *#Love that*

*****

SCENARIO 43: The carpet cleaner gives you an allergy attack.
Have you ever been on vacation at a very touristy hotel? The bedroom carpet smells, and you are sure that they tried to cover it up by using carpet deodorizing powder, but the powder in itself stays heavy in the carpet. It's in the air, and you end up having a sneezing fit. You call the front desk and explain, and you ask for another room. The agent tells you that all rooms are treated with the deodorizing powder. If you have allergies, this is not the hotel for you.

A CUSTOMER COMMENTS
"This is disgusting, because it is not really cleaning; it's just masking."

RATING: You've got to be kidding me@%! | Seriously?! | *OMG!* | Really? | #Love that

WHAT SHOULD HAVE HAPPENED
The front desk should have apologized, and vacuumed and aired out a different room, and offered a room move for the guest. – *#Love that*

*****

SCENARIO 44: You get harassed by the breakfast police.
Have you ever stayed at a hotel where they have a complimentary breakfast? You grab a couple of items and take them up to your spouse in the room. On your way to the room, you are harshly reprimanded and made to appear as if you are stealing.

A CUSTOMER COMMENTS
"I think this continental breakfast is included in my room rate, so I paid for it. Since I have paid for it, I can consume it wherever I wish."

RATING: You've got to be kidding me@%! | Seriously?! | *OMG!* | Really? | #Love that

WHAT SHOULD HAVE HAPPENED
If in fact the hotel did not want you to take the food to your room, a professional sign could be displayed. If someone ignored the sign, just let it go. – *#Love that*

*****

SCENARIO 45: Hotel staff members don't greet you.
You are never greeted or welcomed as you repeatedly walk in and out of the hotel, where you are staying for 4 days.

A CUSTOMER COMMENTS
"Aren't hotels supposed to be your home away from home?"

RATING: You've got to be kidding me@%! | Seriously?! | *OMG!* | Really? | #Love that

WHAT SHOULD HAVE HAPPENED
Valet and bellmen are front line greeters at a hotel. They are the ones that truly know when you are coming and going. Next up is concierge and the front desk agents. All four departments are responsible for providing a warm welcome to all who enter, each and every time a guests comes through the door. – *#Love that*

*****

SCENARIO 46: You're locked out, and no one will help.

You accidentally lock yourself out of your room when you went down the hall for ice. You see a staff member in the hall and ask for assistance, since you are not dressed appropriately to go down to the front desk. They simply refuse to help you.

A CUSTOMER COMMENTS

"I totally get that the staff can't just open the room for anyone... They should at least put some procedure in place, as this happens more often than we think."

RATING: You've got to be kidding me@%! | Seriously?! | OMG! | *Really?* | #Love that

WHAT SHOULD HAVE HAPPENED

Usually, staff is on radio. A simple call placed to security or the front desk, to come and assist the guests, would be ideal. – *#Love that*

*****

SCENARIO 47: The vending machine eats your money.
You go to the vending machine on your floor for a bottle of water, and the machine eats your money. You go back to your room and call the front desk to report the problem. The front desk replies, "Yeah, the machines do that sometimes. Would you like me to connect you to room service so that you can order something to drink?"

A CUSTOMER COMMENTS
"Umm, how about sending me up a bottle of water, since the machine drank my money."

RATING: You've got to be kidding me@%! | Seriously?! | *OMG!* | Really? | #Love that

WHAT SHOULD HAVE HAPPENED
First and foremost, an apology should be offered. Since the front desk is aware of the faulty machines, have a bottle of water sent up right away. – *#Love that*

*****

SCENARIO 48: The cleaning staff ignore the "do not disturb" sign.

Have you ever been exhausted from a long trip and a late check-in the night before? You wake up starving, decide to eat breakfast in the room, and then go right back to sleep. You put the "do not disturb" sign on your door, only to wake up and find a hotel staff person in your room anyway.

A CUSTOMER COMMENTS

"If the signs says stay out, you stay out. To have a complete stranger in your room, without your knowledge, is a personal violation."

RATING: *You've got to be kidding me@%!* | Seriously?! |OMG! | Really? | #Love that

WHAT SHOULD HAVE HAPPENED

This one is pretty easy. Hotel staff are not allowed to break a DND unless it is an emergency, or the rooming list shows that the guest has already checked out. If a staff member ever enters a room and finds a guest asleep, they should turn around and leave the room immediately. – *#Love that*

*****

SCENARIO 49: Your room service order is wrong.

Have you ever ordered from room service, and the order that arrives is incorrect? It then takes another 20 minutes to get some of the correct items, while the first items that arrived are cold.

A CUSTOMER COMMENTS

"This really just ruins the meal all together."

RATING: You've got to be kidding me@%! | Seriously?! | OMG! | ***Really?*** | #Love that

WHAT SHOULD HAVE HAPPENED

First, an apology. Second, ask the guest if they would like to start on the items they have, or if you should just redo the entire order. – *#Love that*

*****

SCENARIO 50: Housekeeping doesn't deliver as promised.

Have you ordered something from housekeeping, and it never comes up?

A CUSTOMER COMMENTS

"I have to tell you that this has never happened to me. How can something never come up? Someone will get a call 15 minutes after it was supposed to be there, and then I give them another 15 minutes to get it, right?"

RATING: You've got to be kidding me@%! | **Seriously?!** | OMG! | Really? | #Love that

WHAT SHOULD HAVE HAPPENED

When housekeeping gets a call from a room, it should be logged. Someone from that department is dispatched to handle the request. When it is done, they notify the department as to who closed out the request. – *#Love that*

*****

SCENARIO 51: The cab that the hotel called for you is late.

Have you ever used the hotel for transportation, and wished you hadn't? You are trying to be prepared, so you ask the night before about a taxi for early the next morning. The front desk agent said, "No problem, just come down; it should take about 15 minutes. So you go down the next morning, and it takes 45 minutes. The front desk agent, who ordered the cab, tells you that if you are not happy with the wait, then call the cab company yourself.

A CUSTOMER COMMENTS

"Did you really just say that out loud?"

RATING: *You've got to be kidding me@%!* | Seriously?! |OMG! | Really? | #Love that

WHAT SHOULD HAVE HAPPENED

How about starting off with an apology? That's always a good start. How about asking your manager if there is another company you can call, since this one is taking much longer than normal? – *#Love that*

*****

SCENARIO 52: The hot breakfast you were promised is denied.
Have you ever stayed at a hotel that includes breakfast with the room rate? You get up the first morning, head down with your breakfast voucher, and go to the restaurant for a nice hot breakfast. The restaurant staff informs you that the voucher is only good for a continental breakfast. You explain to the server that you just spoke with the front desk, and they confirmed that it was for a hot breakfast. The server rudely informs you that they are separate from the hotel, and they don't have to honor what the hotel says.

A CUSTOMER COMMENTS
"I love it when this happens: more than one company under the same roof, dealing with the same customer."

RATING: You've got to be kidding me@%! | Seriously?! | *OMG!* | Really? | #Love that

WHAT SHOULD HAVE HAPPENED
The restaurant staff should speak with their manager. They should check out the voucher and speak with the hotel right away to get the situation resolved. – *#Love that*

*****

SCENARIO 53: A private function keeps you up all night.
We have all stayed at hotels when a private function is going on. Sometimes the private function is really loud and goes until the early morning hours. You speak to the hotel manager, expressing that you are a repeat guest and, in the past, have received a credit for the night you were unable to sleep because of an event. This time, the manager responds with, "We appreciate the suggestion," but he would not extend the offer.

A CUSTOMER COMMENTS
"For a hotel manager to think that it's more important to keep one night's rate, and lose a customer that has stayed multiple nights, seems like really bad customer service, and that management obviously doesn't care about repeat guests."

RATING: You've got to be kidding me@%! | Seriously?! | *OMG!* | Really? | #Love that

WHAT SHOULD HAVE HAPPENED
The manager should have offered an apology and looked up the guest's name to see if, in fact, they really were a repeat guest. If so, offer them the comp. – *#Love that*

*****

SCENARIO 54: The pool is booked for a private function—two days in a row.

Have you gone to a hotel for a long weekend, and then you head to the pool for your daily afternoon swim, but it is booked for a private function? You are disappointed, but you find something else to do, and you put off the swim for the next day. Well, the next day, you go down, and there is another private function. No discount is offered for not being able to use this amenity.

A CUSTOMER COMMENTS

"If it happens one day, I am disappointed, but I will get over it. If it happens two days in a row, then that tells me that the hotel does not care about their guests."

RATING: You've got to be kidding me@%! | Seriously?! | *OMG!* | Really? | #Love that

WHAT SHOULD HAVE HAPPENED

Hotels should not book events back to back that take away amenities and public spaces. You have to realize that you are affecting the same guest. Compensation should be offered. – #Love that

*****

SCENARIO 55: The valet dings your car.

We have all sent our car to valet. You get your car, and they have dinged the very expensive paint job. The manager informs you that they will check the security footage and see what they find. They come back and tell you that they didn't see anything on the footage. You know the ding was not there when you arrived at the hotel, so you ask to see the footage but never receive a response. You are surprised at the lack of truthfulness or desire to make it right.

A CUSTOMER COMMENTS

"When you are leaving the hotel, you don't walk around the car to check for any damage. When you are staying at a five-star hotel, you tell yourself that they see the most beautiful cars all the time."

RATING: You've got to be kidding me@%! | *Seriously?!* | OMG! | Really? | #Love that

WHAT SHOULD HAVE HAPPENED

This is a tough one, as most hotels partner with an outside company to handle their valet. These employees should be trained with the same customer service as the hotel they work for. They could have compromised on the repairs to the paint job. – *#Love that*

*****

SCENARIO 56: The bed has bedbugs.

Have you experienced the dreadful bed bug bites? They are all over your body. You go to the doctor, and he confirms that they are from bed bugs. You call the hotel to inform them of the situation, and you give them your room number, but they seem uninterested. You are put on hold a couple of times, and then you are told to call back and ask to speak to the director of housekeeping.

A CUSTOMER COMMENTS

"How about I just speak with the general manager instead?"

RATING: *You've got to be kidding me@%!* | Seriously?! | OMG! | Really? | #Love that

WHAT SHOULD HAVE HAPPENED

First and foremost, offer an apology. Ask if everyone is alright, and let the guest know that you will look into this. Ask for the room number and the dates of their stay. Let them know that someone will call them back to follow up—and actually follow up with them. If you discover that you indeed have bed bugs, get the room treated immediately, and offer the guest a discount on their rate. – *#Love that*

*****

SCENARIO 57: The Wi-Fi doesn't work.

Have you ever had to use the hotel Wi-Fi for work? You are informed by the staff at check-in that there is free Wi-Fi in the public areas. You try it, and when it doesn't work, you ask the staff for help. Rather than trying to help, their response is that it seems to be working for everyone else.

A CUSTOMER COMMENTS
"Great way to solve problems."

RATING: You've got to be kidding me@%! | Seriously?! | OMG! | ***Really?*** | #Love that

WHAT SHOULD HAVE HAPPENED
The front desk agent should have reviewed the instructions for signing on to the hotel Wi-Fi. If guests are still having issues, find a member on the team who can assist further. – *#Love that*

*****

SCENARIO 58: The pool is full of non-hotel guests.

Have you ever booked a fun weekend at a hotel, and you get there and realize that the pool is filled with non-hotel guests, and some hotel guests are turned away and not able to enjoy the pool?

A CUSTOMER COMMENTS

"I believe the pool is an amenity included in the room rate."

RATING: You've got to be kidding me@%! | Seriously?! | *OMG!* | Really? | #Love that

WHAT SHOULD HAVE HAPPENED

Hotels are starting to do this more and more. They are letting in the public for a cool pool scene. The hotels that decide to go with this approach have to put procedures in place to make sure that they are accommodating their true customer. – *#Love that*

*****

SCENARIO 59: You don't get your wakeup call.

Have you set a wakeup call with the front desk and never received it? No apology was offered. All you received was a simple, "I am not sure what happened."

A CUSTOMER COMMENTS

"I can't believe they didn't acknowledge their error."

RATING: You've got to be kidding me@%! | Seriously?! | **OMG!** | Really? | #Love that

WHAT SHOULD HAVE HAPPENED

First and foremost, an apology should be offered. Next, ask the question, "Is there anything we can do?" – *#Love that*

*****

SCENARIO 60: A simple request goes wrong.

Have you ever stayed in a suite with a wonderful bathtub, and you call down and request bath salts? Time goes by and they still haven't arrived, so you call down again. They take another 15 minutes and then sent up salt—table salt.

A CUSTOMER COMMENTS

"I did say I was taking a bath."

RATING: You've got to be kidding me@%! | Seriously?! | ***OMG!*** | Really? | #Love that

WHAT SHOULD HAVE HAPPENED

It is important to fully understand the request from the guest. It is always best practice to repeat the request to make sure you have it right. – *#Love that*

*****

SCENARIO 61: There's a party in the next room.

Have you ever been in your room, and there is a serious party going on next door? You keep calling downstairs, and you hear security at your neighbor's door. As soon as security leaves, they crank it up again. You do your best to just get through the night. At check-out, you explain the situation, and you are told, "Oh, that's awful. We get partiers every now and then. Was everything else okay?"

A CUSTOMER COMMENTS

"That's it? That's all you've got?"

RATING: You've got to be kidding me@%! | Seriously?! | *OMG!* | Really? | #Love that

WHAT SHOULD HAVE HAPPENED

Hotels should have a policy that when a room receives several complaints due to excessive partying and disrupting other guests, they get one or possibly two warnings to quiet down, and then they are removed from the hotel. *– #Love that*

*****

DEPARTURE

SCENARIO 62: Everything goes wrong.

Every now and then, you stay at a hotel, and everything seems to go wrong—bad check-in, dirty room, a/c doesn't work, and on and on. You can't believe that out of your four-day stay, you have had a different problem with service each day. At check-out, you asked to speak to a manager. The answer you get is, "Well, you should speak up sooner next time."

A CUSTOMER COMMENTS

"Next time? What makes you think there will be a next time with that comment?"

RATING: You've got to be kidding me@%! | *Seriously?!* | OMG! | Really? | #Love that

WHAT SHOULD HAVE HAPPENED

First and foremost, they should offer an apology. They shouldn't tell you what to do when you have a complaint; they should listen. – *#Love that*

*****

SCENARIO 63: The hotel won't own up to its mistakes.

Have you ever had several bad experiences at a hotel, but you are slammed with work, so instead of relocating, you stay and do your best to just deal with it? You inform the front desk every time you have an issue, so that it can get resolved. On your last morning, your room service preorder is not delivered at the scheduled time, and you have to leave. When checking out, you recap all of the issues, and you are told, "We've done a lot for you; what more do you expect?"

A CUSTOMER COMMENTS

"I expect things to go smoothly. I expect professionalism, graciousness, and helpfulness at all times. I expect you to resolve my issues quickly. That's what I expect."

RATING: *You've got to be kidding me@%!* | Seriously?! | OMG! | Really? | #Love that

WHAT SHOULD HAVE HAPPENED

First and foremost, offer an apology. As stated, several things went wrong during this stay. Make sure that the compensation fits the bill for all of the inconveniences the guest has endured.
– #Love that

*****

SCENARIO 64: You get charged for damage that you didn't cause.

Have you ever been charged for damage to a room that was not caused by you? When you check in, you drop your bags and head out for a meeting. When you return later that evening, you immediately notice a stain on a chair, and you refuse to stay in the room. You call down and explain, and they gladly move you. When you go to check out, you are presented with a bill for the damaged chair. You explain what happened. The front desk agent assures you that they would never check someone into a room with damage like that, and you should have reported it immediately after entering the room.

A CUSTOMER COMMENTS

"Since when is it the guest's responsibility to inspect a hotel room and report damage within a certain period of time in order to not be charged for it? If I had reported it in 1 hour rather than 5, would I have not been charged?"

RATING: *You've got to be kidding me@%!* | Seriously?! |OMG! | Really? | #Love that

WHAT SHOULD HAVE HAPPENED

The staff member should have apologized for any confusion. Rather than accuse a guest of lying, let them know that they will need to investigate, and get back to the client shortly**.** – *#Love that*

*****

SCENARIO 65: The bellman is MIA.

During check-out, you ask for your bags to be brought out, as they were being held by the bell staff. You arrange for this with the bellman, about 15 minutes before your pick-up is scheduled. However, it took over 35 minutes to finally receive your bags. You and your driver had to wait, and you never received an apology. You are only told that the bellman was not at his post, or was busy.

A CUSTOMER COMMENTS No one else can help???

"I can't believe that no one else could assist. Show me where the closet is, and I will go in and get my own bags."

RATING: You've got to be kidding me@%! | Seriously?! | *OMG!* | Really? | #Love that

WHAT SHOULD HAVE HAPPENED

If all the bellmen are on calls, then the front desk manager can assist with getting luggage. It does not make sense to have a guest standing around waiting for a specific person to come downstairs, just to pull the luggage out of the closet that is usually located close to the front desk. – *#Love that*

*****

SCENARIO 66: A staff member steals your clothes.

Have you ever come back to your room to find your sheets turned down and some of your clothes missing? You call the manager and explain the situation, and he assures you that no one on his team would ever take clothes from a guest's room.

A CUSTOMER COMMENTS

"That's it? You not going to even start an investigation?"

RATING: *You've got to be kidding me@%!* | Seriously?! |OMG! | Really? | #Love that

WHAT SHOULD HAVE HAPPENED

First and foremost, offer an apology. Inform the guest that you will get security and investigate this immediately. *– #Love that*

*****

Chapter 4

Retailers – Are You Ready?

"Every moment contains an opportunity to create feelings of satisfaction and excitement in a customer. It's up to retailers to make it happen."
– Neil Blumenthal

If you are anything like me, you love to shop! I shop everywhere, from clothing stores, hardware stores, electronic stores, outlet stores, high-end stores, discount stores, etc…

Sometimes I don't think employees truly understand the simple definition of customer service. Customer service is the provision of service to customers—before, during, and after a purchase. I love the show, *Undercover Boss*. I think it is awesome when the top dog comes in to see why his company's revenue isn't where it could be. Take a look at some of the employees that you have on the front lines, selling your products and delivering (or not delivering) good service. Perhaps more bosses should go undercover.

ARRIVAL

SCENARIO 67: The store fails to call you back as promised.
Have you ever been on the phone with a representative, and they promise you a call back to see if everything has been resolved? You never hear from them again.

A CUSTOMER COMMENTS:
"This is a common occurrence of poor or no follow-through. Customers hear this and, too often, the call does not come as promised. Nothing is more infuriating than lack of follow-up when someone is trying to have an issue resolved."

RATING: You've got to be kidding me@%! | Seriously?! | OMG! | ***Really?*** | #Love that

WHAT SHOULD HAVE HAPPENED
Follow up promptly according to your promise. – *#Love that*

*****

SCENARIO 68: The sales associate leaves you hanging.
Have you ever been in the middle of being helped by a representative over the phone, and then she literally starts talking to a coworker, gives him a hug, and talks to him for 10 seconds? She never places you on hold, and you hear the entire exchange.

A CUSTOMER COMMENTS:
"I didn't know what to say. I can recall every piece of that conversation."

RATING: ***You've got to be kidding me@%!*** | Seriously?! |OMG! | Really? | #Love that

WHAT SHOULD HAVE HAPPENED
The representative should have finished the call she was on before catching up with her colleague. If the representative was so inclined that she had to speak with her colleague at that moment, she could have put the call on hold. *– #Love that*

*****

SCENARIO 69: The sales associates say nothing but "hello" and "bye."

You know how you walk into a store, and you get the fake hello; and then, after looking around, and you are walking out, you get the fake goodbye? It's actually delivered in between the conversation that the two sales associates are having at the far end of the store.

A CUSTOMER COMMENTS:

"I personally would rather you not say anything at all. It's just awkward. I know that you don't really care; I can hear it in your voice. It pisses me off, so I don't want to respond, but I feel rude if I don't."

RATING: You've got to be kidding me@%! | Seriously?! | OMG! | *Really?* | #Love that

WHAT SHOULD HAVE HAPPENED

If you are going to welcome someone walking into your store, you should be standing in close proximity to the door. Make sure you make eye contact. – *#Love that*

*****

SCENARIO 70: You are put on hold—forever.
Have you ever been on the phone and listened to this for 20 minutes: "Your call is very important to us; please continue to hold?"

A CUSTOMER COMMENTS:
"My call is obviously not that important, or you would get more people to answer the phones."

RATING: You've got to be kidding me@%! | Seriously?! | OMG! | *Really?* | #Love that

WHAT SHOULD HAVE HAPPENED
This is a tough one. It is obvious that companies cannot keep up with the customer issues. They even farm the services out to other countries. They don't properly train the representatives, and the wait times are longer and longer. – *#Love that*

*****

SCENARIO 71: The customer service department is a nightmare.

Have you called customer service for assistance on a service you purchased, and you are transferred over and over and over again. Not only is this a problem, but to add insult to injury, the last person you spoke to never passes on any information, so you have to keep repeating yourself.

A CUSTOMER COMMENTS:

"First, I am irritated, because once I key in my account number, you should already see all of my information. But it appears that I only key in my information to get past the automated phone guard. Once I am through, my information goes into Never Never Land."

RATING: You've got to be kidding me@%! | Seriously?! | *OMG!* | Really? | #Love that

WHAT SHOULD HAVE HAPPENED

Someone should rewrite the proceeds on how to handle customers over the phone. If you need to make a transfer, take an extra 30 seconds and explain to the next agent what the conversation is, so that when they get on the phone, the customer can be addressed by their name, and their account information is already pulled up and on the screen. – *#Love that*

*****

SCENARIO 72: You're on the phone with robots, not humans.

Have you ever been on the phone, and you can't speak with a live person? Every company seems to want to have a different code word to get directly to a live representative: operator, representative, agent, live agent, etc....

A CUSTOMER COMMENTS:

"I love it when they tell you what the secret password is, and when you use it, you get the automated robot guy again, saying, "To help direct you to the live agent, tell me what you are calling about." You say, "Billing." The robot comes back and says, "I can help you with billing." Ugh! "Live agent, live agent, live agent!"

RATING: You've got to be kidding me@%! | Seriously?! | OMG! | *Really?* | #Love that

WHAT SHOULD HAVE HAPPENED

Companies should let you press 0. *— #Love that*

*****

SCENARIO 73: The store misleads you with false advertising.
Have you ever bought something on sale, and the sale price is not honored at the register? There are sale items labelled all over the store. When you go to customer service about it, they will give you the advertised price, but they make NO attempt to fix the problem by removing the false advertising.

A CUSTOMER COMMENTS:
"Since I am a big shopper, I am always watching the register. You have to make sure that you are not being over charged."

RATING: You've got to be kidding me@%! | Seriously?! | OMG! | *Really?* | #Love that

WHAT SHOULD HAVE HAPPENED
First and foremost, apologize for the mistake, and honor the sales price. Afterwards, you should call a manager over to make them aware of the problem so that it can get fixed, because it is bound to happen to more customers. – *#Love that*

*****

SCENARIO 74: You get stuck on hold with a lot of other unhappy customers.

It is scary to hear, "We are experiencing heavy call volumes at this time. You can stay on hold or call back."

A CUSTOMER COMMENTS:

"This means that a lot of people are having the same issue you are."

RATING: You've got to be kidding me@%! | Seriously?! | *OMG!* | Really? | #Love that

WHAT SHOULD HAVE HAPPENED

It is obvious that the company cannot keep up with the customer issues. – *#Love that*

*****

DURING THE SHOP

SCENARIO 75: The sales associates ignore you.
Have you ever gone up to the check-out counter with the items you want to purchase, and the sales associate is involved in a conversation with her colleague? Neither of them even acknowledges that you are standing at the counter. They do their best NOT to make eye contact with you until they are done with their juicy story.

A CUSTOMER COMMENTS:
"I see me standing here. That story must be really juicy, since you are not stopping to come and assist me."

RATING: You've got to be kidding me@%! | Seriously?! | OMG! | ***Really?*** | #Love that

WHAT SHOULD HAVE HAPPENED
As soon as the associates noticed a customer walking their way, they should have stopped talking. An associate should have met the customer at the counter and been ready to assist. – *#Love that*

*****

SCENARIO 76: The sales associate insults you.

You are shopping with a friend in one of the lingerie stores. You both are a little overweight. You see a really nice bra and panty set, and you say, "They should make this in plus sizes; they would sell more. I would totally buy this set." You then hear the manager say under her breath, "Maybe if you lose some weight, we would have things that fit you."

A CUSTOMER COMMENTS:

"Are you even human? Do you have any feelings?"

RATING: *You've got to be kidding me@%!* | Seriously?! |OMG! | Really? | #Love that

WHAT SHOULD HAVE HAPPENED

If you work with clients or customers in any role, you need to care about the problems they want solved. Show it by taking positive action to help them out. – *#Love that*

*****

SCENARIO 77: The sales associate sends you on a wild goose chase.

Have you ever been looking for an item, and the clerk sends you to the wrong location in the store.

A CUSTOMER COMMENTS:

"Do you even work here? How can you send me in the wrong direction?"

RATING: You've got to be kidding me@%! | ***Seriously?!*** | OMG! | Really? | #Love that

WHAT SHOULD HAVE HAPPENED

The associate should have walked you over to the item. – *#Love that*

*****

SCENARIO 78: The customer service rep expects you to do her job.

You are shopping with a deadline, so when you walk into the store, you go straight to the customer service counter and ask for the item you are looking for. The representative waves her arm in the direction you need to go, and says, "Over there." As you walk away, you hear her turn to her co-worker and say, "She didn't even TRY to find it on her own."

A CUSTOMER COMMENTS:
"Uh, isn't that what you are there for?"

RATING: You've got to be kidding me@%! | *Seriously?!* | OMG! | Really? | #Love that

WHAT SHOULD HAVE HAPPENED
First and foremost, you should never talk about a customer on the floor in earshot of other customers—especially the customer you are talking about! – *#Love that*

*****

SCENARIO 79: The sales clerks are unwilling to right a wrong.
Have you ever been shopping in a high-end leather goods store, and they take forever to acknowledge you? By the time they pay attention to you, you have made your selection to purchase a pair of sunglasses. After returning home, you find that they have given you the wrong pair. You call them to inform them of their mistake. They tell you that you should have checked prior to leaving the store, and that it is your mistake. In addition, the frame you intended to buy is now sold out. They will not exchange, nor find a pair and have them shipped, as is customary for this caliber of company.

A CUSTOMER COMMENTS:
"Have you lost your mind? You can only imagine how much these glasses cost, and this is the type of treatment you are getting."

RATING: *You've got to be kidding me@%!* | Seriously?! | OMG! | Really? | #Love that

WHAT SHOULD HAVE HAPPENED
First and foremost, offer an apology. Second, take care of the exchange for the customer. – *#Love that*

*****

SCENARIO 80: The sales associates are all MIA.
No one is around, and you have to hunt someone down for help. You think you found the item you want, but you have questions about it.

A CUSTOMER COMMENTS:
"Aren't the sales associates supposed to visible on the floor to help customers and make sales?"

RATING: You've got to be kidding me@%! | Seriously?! | OMG! | ***Really?*** | #Love that

WHAT SHOULD HAVE HAPPENED
Hopefully, this customer was greeted at the door. There should be sales associates walking around, making sure that merchandise is presentable, and seeing if there are any customers that need assistance. – *#Love that*

*****

SCENARIO 81: You're being profiled.

Have you ever had a sales clerk following you around the store and just loitering behind you?

A CUSTOMER COMMENTS:

"That's annoying. They are following you around for one of two reasons. One, they really want to sell you something. As soon as you pick up a shirt, they are going to tell you how fabulous it is and that you should buy it. Or, they are profiling you, and as soon as you pick up that shirt, they are watching to make sure you don't put it in your purse."

RATING: You've got to be kidding me@%! | ***Seriously?!*** | OMG! | Really? | #Love that

WHAT SHOULD HAVE HAPPENED

When a good sales associate approaches you and asks you if you need assistance, and you tell them that you are just looking right now, they should respectfully say, "If you need me for anything, I will be right over there." Now you know where they are in case you need their help. – *#Love that*

*****

SCENARIO 82: The store is filthy.

Have you ever been shopping in one of the discount stores, and they are just filthy? So, you think maybe they just forgot to sweep and mop. You go back to the store the next weekend (to make a return J), and the same large dust balls are still there.

A CUSTOMER COMMENTS:

"This is just disgusting."

RATING: You've got to be kidding me@%! | Seriously?! | **OMG!** | Really? | #Love that

WHAT SHOULD HAVE HAPPENED

This is simple. The store should be cleaned each night and throughout the day as needed. You want your store to be presentable for your customers. No one wants to shop and spend time in a dirty store. – *#Love that*

*****

SCENARIO 83: The sales associate gives up too easily.

Have you ever been shopping, and the store is sold out of the item you want? The clerk just asks if there is anything else you need?

A CUSTOMER COMMENTS:

"Yes, I need the item I came in here to buy. I want the item, and I am willing to spend money. I thought sales people were supposed to make sales."

RATING: You've got to be kidding me@%! | Seriously?! | OMG! | ***Really?*** | #Love that

WHAT SHOULD HAVE HAPPENED

The associate should ask if you would like him to check another store, or if you would like him to check online for you. – *#Love that*

*****

SCENARIO 84: Long lines. One cashier. You do the math.
Have you ever been in long lines in a clothing store, and there is only one cashier? There are an abundant of coworkers stocking shelves around the store, but just one cashier. And to top it off, the cashier appears to be afraid to call for backup.

A CUSTOMER COMMENTS:
"You do your best to make direct eye contact with the one cashier, to give her the look that you can't believe you are waiting in this line with only one cashier—the look that says, "Do something already, and call for more cashiers to get this line moving. Now!" (You know the look.)

RATING: You've got to be kidding me@%! | Seriously?! | ***OMG!*** | Really? | #Love that

WHAT SHOULD HAVE HAPPENED
Companies should have a standard rule that if you have so many people in line, automatically add another cashier. Customers will walk in and walk right out of a store if the line is too long. – *#Love that*

*****

SCENARIO 85: The sales associate is completely untrained.
Have you ever asked a sales associate for help, only to find out that they are not knowledgeable to assist you? They are polite enough to listen to your full question, and then have no idea how to help you.

A CUSTOMER COMMENTS:
"Why are you even on the floor out here to assist customers, when you do not have the knowledge?"

RATING: You've got to be kidding me@%! | Seriously?! | OMG! | *Really?* | #Love that

WHAT SHOULD HAVE HAPPENED
Sales associates have to go through a proper training process so that they have adequate knowledge on the products they are selling. – *#Love that*

*****

SCENARIO 86: The sales associates ignore you.
Have you every walked through a store and noticed a lot of employees stocking shelves. Not one person acknowledges you, greets you, or smiles at you. If you spend money in a store, you want to be acknowledged.

A CUSTOMER COMMENTS:
"What happened to common courtesy?"

RATING: You've got to be kidding me@%! | Seriously?! | OMG! | *Really?* | #Love that

WHAT SHOULD HAVE HAPPENED
What happened to the 10/5 rule? At 10 feet, you make eye contact. At 5 feet, you say hello. You could also greet the customer and ask if they are finding everything okay. – *#Love that*

*****

SCENARIO 87: The customer service rep isn't empowered to help.

How crazy is it that when you call customer service, and you are trying to be efficient with your time, you immediately ask for a supervisor. The agent won't transfer you until you explain why you are calling. After you explain, she is not empowered to resolve your problem, and needs to transfer you to her supervisor.

A CUSTOMER COMMENTS:

"Okay, that's who I asked for at the beginning of my call."

RATING: You've got to be kidding me@%! | Seriously?! | *OMG!* | Really? | #Love that

WHAT SHOULD HAVE HAPPENED

There should be ongoing training so that more lower-level agents can assist with more of the issues coming in. – *#Love that*

*****

SCENARIO 88: The sales associate is sick.

Have you ever been helped by a sick sales associate? They are coughing and sneezing, and it is very clear that it is not allergies.

A CUSTOMER COMMENTS:

"I don't know about you, but I am a germaphobe. I don't want to handle anything that this associate has just touched."

RATING: You've got to be kidding me@%! | Seriously?! | **OMG!** | Really? | #Love that

WHAT SHOULD HAVE HAPPENED

This is an easy one. If you are sick, do not go to work. If your manager sees that you are sick, he should send you home. – *#Love that*

*****

SCENARIO 89: The sales associate gives bogus reasons for not taking your return.

Have you ever gone to a high-end leather goods store, and you purchase a purse in a smaller size because the larger size you want is sold out? Immediately after you buy it, you call another store, and they have the larger size. You rush over to the store and ask to exchange the one you have, for the larger size. The sales associate tells you that she can't because the one you have is damaged. You tell her that you literally just bought it from another store and drove straight over there, and now you ask for the manager. You tell the manager to call the store that you just came from.

A CUSTOMER COMMENTS:

"Are you for real? I am bringing you the purse that I just purchased from your sister store."

RATING: You've got to be kidding me@%! | Seriously?! | OMG! | *Really?* | #Love that

WHAT SHOULD HAVE HAPPENED

First, offer an apology for any miscommunication. If you feel the need to verify that it was just purchased, just look at the receipt. Do the exchange, and keep the customer happy. – *#Love that*

*****

SCENARIO 90: You can't get a return on an obviously faulty item.

Have you ever bought something from an outlet store that had "final sale" on it? You then get home and discover that the pair of shoes you bought are actually two different sizes? Your first thought is, "I can't believe I have to drive all the way back to the outlet." You finally drive out the next weekend, and you explain the problem to the sales clerk. She informs you that it was a final sale and that she cannot do a return.

A CUSTOMER COMMENTS:

"Uh, you sold me an item that I can't use. I see that it was a mistake, and I had to drive all the way back out here. Take some responsibility for this error."

RATING: *You've got to be kidding me@%!* | Seriously?! | OMG! | Really? | #Love that

WHAT SHOULD HAVE HAPPENED

First and foremost, offer an apology for selling something that cannot possibly be used. Take ownership of the mistake; give the refund, and retain the client. – *#Love that*

*****

SCENARIO 91: How rude?!

A customer calls in to check on her order, and the representative informs her that there has not been any change. The customer enquires further as to why there is a delay. The representative stated that he was sorry, and reminded the customer that he would call if and when he had an update, and that she did not have to keep calling back. The customer asked if the representative could place a call and find out what is going on. After much back and forth, the representative asked if she just wanted to cancel the order, and then she would not have to worry about this anymore.

A CUSTOMER COMMENTS:

"You call to get an update, and the representative won't take the time to find out what is going on. He is telling you that he is just going to wait until he hears something, and so should you."

RATING: *You've got to be kidding me@%!* | Seriously?! |OMG! | Really? | #Love that

WHAT SHOULD HAVE HAPPENED

Place the call to the warehouse, and get the status of the delivery. Then politely call the customer back, extend apologies for the delay, and give her the update she asked for. *– #Love that*

*****

SCENARIO 92: One penny please?

A customer receives a gift, and it is the wrong size. He has the receipt and has not opened any packaging. He picks out the correct size and walks up to the counter. The representative does the exchange and informs him that he owes her a penny. He asked if the merchandise was a different price. The representative stated that it was the same exact price. He asked why he had to pay a penny. The representative said, "I don't know; that's what the computer says," and holds out her hand for the penny.

A CUSTOMER COMMENTS:

"If I exchange an item for a different size, one day after it was purchased, and there is no change in the price of the item, I shouldn't owe you anything at all."

RATING: You've got to be kidding me@%! | *Seriously?!* | OMG! | Really? | #Love that

WHAT SHOULD HAVE HAPPENED

Let the customer know that it does seem strange, and that you will adjust the penny off. – *#Love that*

*****

SCENARIO 93: The sales associate starts airing her personal problems.

Have you ever been shopping over a holiday weekend, with all of the sales going on? The lines at the department stores are so long. You finally get to the counter, and instead of the sales associate apologizing for the wait, she starts complaining that they don't have enough staff on today.

A CUSTOMER COMMENTS:

"I understand that everyone has problems at work. Unfortunately, when you are in the service industry, you can't share the mishaps with the customers. I would have been more than happy to call her boss and express her feelings for her."

RATING: You've got to be kidding me@%! | Seriously?! | *OMG!* | Really? | #Love that

WHAT SHOULD HAVE HAPPENED

First and foremost, offer an apology. Take care of the customers as best you can. Make sure that you speak with your boss about the scheduling, for better customer service. – *#Love that*

*****

SCENARIO 94: The sales associate is "on a break."
Have you ever been shopping, and you finally find a sales associate, and you go through explaining what you are looking for? You are waiting for a helpful response, only to have the associate say, "I am sorry, but I am headed out on my break. You can ask that sales rep over there for help."

A CUSTOMER COMMENTS:
"Well, I am sorry to disturb you."

RATING: You've got to be kidding me@%! | Seriously?! | ***OMG!*** | Really? | #Love that

WHAT SHOULD HAVE HAPPENED
If the sales associate must go on their break at that exact moment, they should get another associate and hand you over.
– *#Love that*

*****

SCENARIO 95: The sales associate slow-walks your return.
You go to the store to return something that does not look flattering on you. The sales associate asks if you found something else. You tell him no and that you just want to make a return. He goes on and on to tell you about all the new dresses that have come in, and that he is happy to show you. You thank him and tell him that you just want to do a return. He keeps persisting that you should look around the store for something else.

A CUSTOMER COMMENTS:
"This is now aggravating. You have asked, and I have answered—3 times. Just do the return."

RATING: You've got to be kidding me@%! | Seriously?! | OMG! | ***Really?*** | #Love that

WHAT SHOULD HAVE HAPPENED
It is the practice of some retail chains to reduce the number of returns, and to get that customer to do an exchange instead. Customer service is about helping the client get what they need. It is not about pressing them into doing something they don't want to do. – *#Love that*

*****

SCENARIO 96: You're treated like one of the "guys."
Have you ever been shopping with the ladies, and the sales associate walks over and greets you with, "Hey, guys."

A CUSTOMER COMMENTS:
"Did he even look at us? We are a bunch of fantastic women!"

RATING: You've got to be kidding me@%! | Seriously?! | OMG! | *Really?* | #Love that

WHAT SHOULD HAVE HAPPENED
Customers should always be addressed professionally and appropriately. – *#Love that*

*****

SCENARIO 97: The sales associate says that her hands are tied.
Have you had something go wrong with your purchase, and you negotiate a discount for all the trouble you had to go through? The representative tells you that she understands what you are asking for, but the system won't let her do that.

A CUSTOMER COMMENTS:
"Actually, you just haven't been trained on how to do that in the system. If you could kindly call someone else over, that would be great."

RATING: You've got to be kidding me@%! | Seriously?! | OMG! | ***Really?*** | #Love that

WHAT SHOULD HAVE HAPPENED
There is always a way to enter a discount in the sales system. If your manager hasn't trained you on this, then call him over to assist. – *#Love that*

*****

SCENARIO 98: The sales associate is lazy.
Have you ever been looking for an item, and the clerk tells you that they don't have it, without even checking. He does not offer to help you find a comparable product. He acts like it was a bother to assist you.

A CUSTOMER COMMENTS:
"Do you really believe him, or do you think he is just lazy?"

RATING: You've got to be kidding me@%! | Seriously?! | OMG! | *Really?* | #Love that

WHAT SHOULD HAVE HAPPENED
He should have apologized that the store was out of stock for your particular item. He should have asked if you wanted to see something comparable or if you wanted him to check another store. – *#Love that*

*****

SCENARIO 99: Not all of your purchases are in the bag.

Have you ever purchased 150 dollars in merchandise and got home to discover that all the items did not make it in your bag? You go back to the store and straight to the cashier that rang you up. The cashier claims she did not ring you up. You explain your situation and notice that the item that was left behind is on the back counter at her register. She still refuses to give you the item even though you show her the receipt. You can't believe this is happening. You only made this purchase about 30 minutes ago. Instead, the cashier is rude and calls the manager and security.

A CUSTOMER COMMENTS:

"No customer should ever be treated and insulted. Give them the benefit of the doubt, and check out their story."

RATING: *You've got to be kidding me@%!* | Seriously?! |OMG! | Really? | #Love that

WHAT SHOULD HAVE HAPPENED

The cashier should have apologized for any confusion. She could have easily checked the receipt, which has the date and time, and most likely the cashier or register number. She then could have scanned the item against the receipt. *– #Love that*

*****

SCENARIO 100: The online Live Chat rep can't help you.
Have you tried using the online Chat for customer service issues? After all the back and forth, you find out that they cannot help you. They are only authorized to do so much. They then offer to have their supervisor call you, but they can't assist either, and you have to speak to someone in another department.

A CUSTOMER COMMENTS:
"Well, that was just a big waste of my time. It was great typing practice, but that was about it."

RATING: You've got to be kidding me@%! | ***Seriously?!*** | OMG! | Really? | #Love that

WHAT SHOULD HAVE HAPPENED
Companies should be upfront and tell you which services the Live Chat can assist with. For all other services, you have to call the customer service number. – *#Love that*

*****

AND LAST BUT NOT LEAST...

SCENARIO 101: You get stuck with a two-by-four.
Have you ever purchased an item, and you take it home and open the box, and then you find a 2x4 inside? You didn't purchase this off the street; it was from one of the biggest chain stores around. You head to the store to return it, only to be told that you wouldn't be able to get a refund or an exchange. At this point, you are livid. You purchased this directly from the store. Someone had to have purchased the item previously and, obviously, returned it with the 2x4.

A CUSTOMER COMMENTS:
"If I get home and open a purchase, and it's a bunch of crap, I am getting a new item or my money back. The store may have been duped, but I am not going to lose my money because of this."

RATING: *You've got to be kidding me@%!* | Seriously?! |OMG! | Really? | #Love that

WHAT SHOULD HAVE HAPPENED
You know this by heart now. First and foremost, offer an apology, and inform the customer that you will have to investigate. – *#Love that*

*****

Chapter 5

Deliver Five Star Service at Any Level

1. Active Listening – Be attentive, and really listen when the customer is speaking.
2. Attentiveness – Pay close attention to the issue being brought to you.
3. Awareness – It is important to read the physical and emotional cues of the customer.
4. Conflict Resolution – Your goal is to take care of the customer and whatever their issue is.
5. Creativity – Think outside the box when resolving issues.
6. Decision Making – If you can't do it, make sure you know who can.
7. Dependability – It is important that the customer quality be trustworthy and reliable.
8. Effective Communicate - Use clear and positive communication when speaking with customers.
9. Empathy – Show that you understand how the customer is feeling about the situation.
10. Friendliness – Make eye contact, introduce yourself, and smile when interacting with guests.
11. Knowledge – Have knowledge of your service or product so you can fully serve the customer.
12. Patience – Take the time to listen and assist the customer with what they need.
13. Responsiveness – It is important to react quickly and positively.
14. Timeliness – Resolve the issue in a timely manner.

Always remember to greet someone as if they were a guest in your own home. And don't forget to thank them for their business. Make sure to wrap up with customer satisfaction.

Chapter 6

Farewell

I hope you have had a fun read.

The sad thing is that all of the SCENARIOs in this book are true. I have experienced over half of them, and the rest are experiences and stories from friends and colleagues.

Customers are looking for genuine greetings, smiling faces, and knowledgeable staff that is available when they need them.

Excellent customer service is directly related to a company's revenue. You can read up on all the stats; a new customer is harder to get, so just retain the ones you already have. Deliver great products and excellent service, and you can't go wrong.

You are entitled to excellent service. You are paying for the product AND the service of receiving it. If you don't feel that you are getting the service you deserve, take your money and go somewhere else!

About the Author

Vivian Campbell lives in Los Angeles, California.

The author is available for delivering keynote presentations to appropriate audiences. For rates and availability, please contact the author directly at service@101wayscustomerservice.com.

To order more books, search for "101ways" on Amazon.com.

Finally, if you have been inspired and entertained by this book, one thing you can do is to always be of service to others. The world needs more hospitality.

Made in the USA
Lexington, KY
18 December 2019